COYOTES

COYOTES

by Cherie Winner

A Carolrhoda Nature Watch Book

 Carolrhoda Books, Inc./Minneapolis

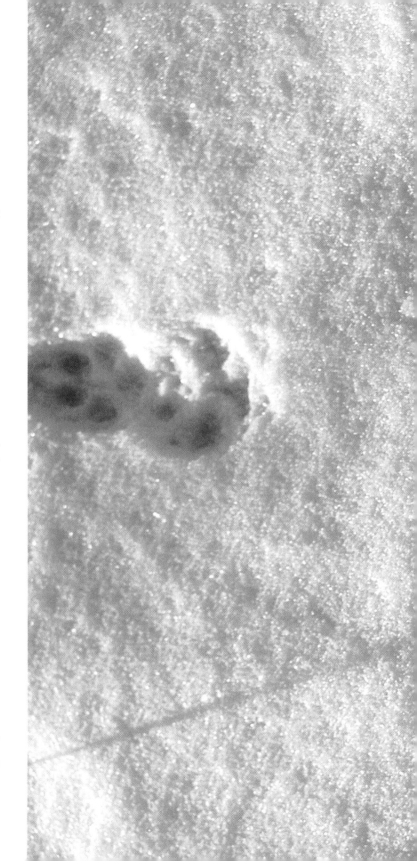

For Bob, who loved all things wild and wonderful

The author thanks Dr. Mollie Matteson, Montana State
University; John L. Weeks, Furbearer Biologist for the state
of Ohio; and Dr. Marc Bekoff, University of Colorado-
Boulder, for sharing their knowledge of coyotes.

This book is available in two editions:
Library binding by Carolrhoda Books, Inc.
Softcover by First Avenue Editions
c/o The Lerner Group
241 First Avenue North, Minneapolis, MN 55401

LIBRARY OF CONGRESS CATALOGING-IN-PUBLICATION DATA

Winner, Cherie.
    Coyotes / by Cherie Winner.
        p.   cm.
    "A Carolrhoda nature watch book."
    Includes index.
    ISBN 0-87614-938-7 (lib. bdg.)
    ISBN 0-87614-957-3 (pbk.)
    1. Coyotes—Juvenile literature. [1. Coyotes.] I. Title.
QL737.C22W55   1995
599.74'442—dc20   94-45585
                                                  CIP
                                                  AC

Manufactured in the United States of America
1 2 3 4 5 6 – JR – 00 99 98 97 96 95

CONTENTS

INTRODUCTION

"Ay-ay-ow-oo!"

As the moon rises over the prairie, the cry of a coyote breaks the silence. Soon another coyote joins in, and then another, until the night is filled with howls.

This haunting sound has both enchanted and frightened people for thousands of years. The Native Americans who first heard coyotes made up myths and legends about them. In some of these stories, coyotes gave humans gifts, such as fire or stars. In other legends, coyotes were pranksters, always trying to show off or cheat someone.

Even now, coyotes are seen both ways. Some people view coyotes as evil creatures who kill other animals just for the fun of it. Other people value coyotes because they keep the number of pesky rodents and rabbits under control.

One thing both sides agree on is that coyotes are smart and **adaptable**. This means they do not have just one way to do things. They are able to learn from their own experiences and by watching other animals. They can invent new ways of hunting or avoiding danger.

Coyotes can even adapt to different ways of living. They are very sociable animals who usually live in a **pack** with other coyotes. Pack members howl, play, and hunt together. They share their food as well as the job of raising pups. But coyotes have also adapted to living alone in areas where human activities such as hunting and trapping make it difficult for a pack to find enough food and stay safe.

Although this pair of coyotes is hunting together, a mouse is too small to share and belongs to the one who catches it.

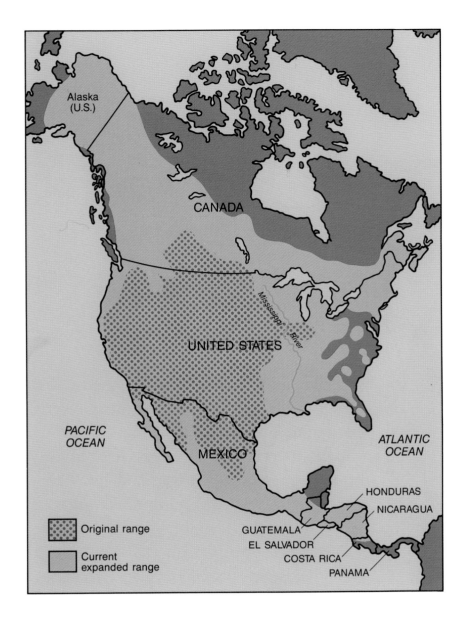

Alaska
(U.S.)

CANADA

Mississippi River

UNITED STATES

PACIFIC
OCEAN

ATLANTIC
OCEAN

MEXICO

HONDURAS
NICARAGUA
GUATEMALA
EL SALVADOR
COSTA RICA
PANAMA

Original range

Current
expanded range

Being adaptable has helped coyotes expand their **range**, or area in which they live. When European explorers first came to America, coyotes lived mainly west of the Mississippi River, on the flat, grassy prairies of the Great Plains. As pioneers began settling on the plains in the 1800s, coyotes quickly learned that farms and towns were good places to find rodents. The grain raised by farmers and the garbage dumped near new towns attracted rats, mice, and ground squirrels, which make up a large portion of the coyote's diet.

Coyotes followed the pioneers away from the prairies and into new **habitats,** such as mountains and forests. They moved north with gold miners headed for the Yukon, and west across the Rocky Mountains with settlers headed for California. Coyotes can now be found from Point Barrow, Alaska, on the Arctic Ocean, all the way to Costa Rica, in Central America.

A coyote is smaller and has redder fur than this wolf.

PHYSICAL CHARACTERISTICS

The name *coyote* (ky-OH-tee or KY-oat) comes from the Aztecs' word *coyotl,* which means "singing dog." Coyotes *(Canis latrans)* are close relatives of gray wolves *(Canis lupus)* and dogs *(Canis familiaris).* All are mammals—animals that **nurse** their young—and all belong to the family Canidae (KAN-uh-dee), which also includes foxes and jackals.

Coyotes resemble wolves but are smaller and more slender. Most adult coyotes stand from 20 to 24 inches (50 to 60 cm) tall at the shoulder and weigh from 20 to 50 pounds (9 to 22.5 kg). Males are usually a bit larger than females. The biggest coyote ever measured was a male from Wyoming who weighed almost 75 pounds (34 kg).

The coyote's coat is cream colored on the chest and belly, and may be golden brown, light gray, dark gray, or reddish on its sides and back. The fur is made up of short, soft **underfur** and longer **guard hairs.** Guard hairs are darker and coarser than the underfur and are usually black at the tips. Water runs right off the guard hairs, so the coyote stays dry. The underfur keeps the coyote warm.

Coyotes have a bushy tail that points straight outward or down toward the ground. Adults have a long, narrow snout and pointed ears. Their feet are smaller than the feet of a similar-sized dog.

Like dogs and wolves, coyotes have teeth that are especially good for eating meat. They have long, strong **canine** (KAY-nine) **teeth** near the front of the mouth, and large cutting teeth called **carnassials** (kar-NASS-ee-uhls) farther back. Canines are especially good for catching and holding **prey** (PRAY), and carnassials are good for tearing meat.

A big yawn reveals this coyote's pointed canine teeth and jagged carnassials.

FINDING A MEAL

Some people who have watched coyotes for years say that a coyote will eat anything once. Coyotes are primarily **carnivores,** or meat eaters. But they are not picky. They may also eat insects, fruits, berries, or grass.

Coyotes do not care how fresh their meat is either. They are both **scavengers** and **predators.** As scavengers, they eat the bodies of animals that other animals have killed or that have died from illness, injury, or old age. The meat of dead animals is called **carrion** (KARE-ee-un). Coyotes will eat carrion that is several days old, even if it has started to rot.

This dead bison is a treasure for a scavenging coyote.

A hungry coyote will eat just about anything, including berries (left) and a sagebrush vole (below).

As predators, coyotes capture and kill live animals. Often two or more pack members will hunt together, but each finds and captures most small prey—mice, birds, ground squirrels, and rabbits—by itself. In packs, they also hunt big game such as elk, deer, and antelope.

A coyote usually hunts in the same area every day. The size of its hunting area depends mostly on how much food is available. Where rabbits and rodents are plentiful, one coyote may cover 2.5 square miles (6.5 km²) to find the food it needs. Where prey are scarce, each coyote may need 10 square miles (26 km²) or more to find the same amount of food.

Coyotes rely on their keen eyesight and hearing to find prey. A coyote on the hunt stops frequently to look and listen for signs of a bird or squirrel scurrying for cover. Coyotes are especially alert to movement. A coyote may walk right past a rabbit who is perfectly still, but if the rabbit moves at all—blinks an eye, flicks an ear—the coyote will see it and be after it in a flash.

The coyote's sharp sense of hearing is most important when it comes to finding and capturing mice. In summer, these tiny rodents scurry through tunnels in the grass, searching for seeds to eat. The coyote cannot see them, but it can hear them. It turns its ears to pick up sounds from all directions and may stand in one spot for many minutes, listening for the little scrapes and squeaks mice make.

Finally a mouse passes close to the coyote, and *Boom!* The coyote leaps into the air and comes down hard on its front paws. The coyote tries to pin the mouse down, then bites through the grass to get at it. If the mouse darts out of the way, the coyote pounces again. The coyote is successful in catching the mouse about half the time.

14

Listening and pouncing skills (opposite page and above) *are valuable when hunting rodents.*

In winter, mice dig tunnels in the snow instead of the grass, but the coyote hunts the same way. It stands quietly, listening for sounds that tell it a mouse is nearby. Deep snow can make it hard to get the mouse on the first try. In fact, in snow the coyote may succeed only once in ten tries.

This coyote probably had help catching a whitetail jackrabbit.

Capturing a jackrabbit is an even tougher job. Jackrabbits are very fast and can outrun a coyote, so two coyotes will often team up. One will take off after the prey while the other sits and watches. The chasing coyote will herd the jackrabbit so that it circles back to where the second coyote is waiting. Just as the first coyote is getting tired, the second coyote takes over the chase and the first one stops to rest. They may switch off several times before the jackrabbit tires and slows down enough to be caught. The two coyotes then share the meal.

Two coyotes near a badger's den hope for an opportunity to catch prairie dogs.

When a coyote sees a badger digging up an entrance to a prairie dog burrow, it waits nearby for a dining opportunity. If the prairie dog darts out of a different hole to escape the badger, the coyote nabs it. If the prairie dog stays in the burrow, the badger will eventually reach it. The coyote and badger do not share their catch, but they may hunt together for several hours, each partner getting plenty to eat.

This kind of cooperation between different kinds of animals is unusual—especially since each is known to attack the other's babies—but it makes sense. Coyotes are fast, but they cannot dig very well. Badgers are great diggers, but they do not run very fast.

17

Sniffing out a meal

To bring down large game, up to twelve coyotes may work together. While some steer the prey, others position themselves to attack. Hunting in packs is considered a sign of intelligence, because it requires good communication and cooperation among the pack members.

Lone coyotes rarely attack healthy adult deer, elk, or antelope. These animals defend themselves by striking out with their hooves. Sometimes they even kill coyotes. If an animal that large faces a coyote instead of running away, the coyote usually backs off.

If packs are too small to attack deer or elk successfully, they may turn to livestock, especially sheep. Sheep are not as smart or aggressive as wild game and are easier for coyotes to kill. However, most coyotes avoid livestock. They seem to prefer wild game.

18

Bringing down a snowshoe hare

Biologists estimate that an adult coyote needs to eat at least 1.3 pounds (0.59 kg) of meat each day to stay healthy. This is equal to about 13 mice every day or one jackrabbit every five days.

But like many carnivores, coyotes do not always eat regularly. If a coyote has gone for days without food, it may gulp down up to 20 pounds (9 kg) of meat in half an hour. After such a huge meal, the coyote will not need to eat again for several days.

What coyotes eat depends on what season it is and what food is available. Rabbits and mice are favorite prey year-round. In spring, coyotes also eat birds that nest on or near the ground, such as grouse and quail. Ground squirrels and prairie dogs are a major food source from late spring to early fall.

Being part of a pack is an advantage during the cold winter months because members work together to find food and keep warm.

Cold weather is hard on all wild animals, and many deer, elk, and antelope die. The carrion of these animals makes up about a third of the coyote's diet during the winter. When one member of a pack finds a large **carcass**, or dead animal, it howls to tell other pack members about the treasure it has found. Biologists have watched a pack of coyotes savor an elk carcass for many days, chasing away members of other packs. When they finally finish eating the carcass, they move on to find other sources of food.

PACK LIFE

A well-organized pack like the one savoring the elk carcass is almost always a family. The leaders, called the **alpha** (AL-fuh) male and alpha female, raise a family of pups each year. The alphas are the only members of the pack who reproduce. Most other members of the pack are relatives of the alpha pair: brothers or sisters, aunts or uncles, or offspring from previous years. A few unrelated coyotes may also be accepted into the pack. Among the non-alpha coyotes, some are more **dominant,** or higher ranking, than others. But the alpha pair ranks higher than all the others.

In areas where they are not hunted or trapped by humans, packs are usually large, with up to twelve adult members. Coyotes that are actively hunted by humans tend to live alone or in small packs so they can hide more easily. A small coyote pack may consist of just the alpha male and female and their young pups.

The top dogs in a pack are always the alpha male and the alpha female (left). The ranks of the rest of the pack members are determined by displays of aggression (above).

Members of a pack communicate with each other by gestures and vocal signals. They use much of the same body language that dogs do. When they greet other members of their family, they wag their tails. To invite another coyote to play, they bow down and stretch out their front legs. When the members of a pack are separated from each other, they communicate by howling. This is how they tell each other where they are and whether or not they have found food.

Coyotes also use odors to communicate. Members of a pack mark their **territory,** or area where they live, by urinating on bushes, rocks, or trees along its border. When other coyotes smell this, they know that a pack has claimed the area.

Usually other coyotes will avoid a marked territory. But if they are hungry, they may venture in to search for food. If a resident coyote sees this, it will chase the intruder away.

This rolling land provides plenty of places for coyotes to hide.

The size of the territory needed by a pack of coyotes depends mostly on the size of the pack and how much food is available. It also depends on whether the land is flat or hilly. Territories in hilly country can be smaller than those on flat land because there are more places to hide. Coyotes like to be hidden from the view of other coyotes, especially when their pups are very young.

Much of pack life revolves around the pups—protecting them, feeding them, and teaching them the skills they will need to survive on their own. While adult coyotes are very skillful hunters, the pups have to be taught how to find, stalk, and capture prey. Most members of the pack contribute to the pups' care and education. But the alphas—the pups' parents—are still their most important teachers.

COURTSHIP AND MATING

The alpha coyotes form very close bonds with their offspring and each other. The couple will stay together their entire lives, so choosing a mate is serious business. Coyote **courtship** begins in late December or early January. During courtship, female coyotes who have no partner choose a male to mate with. Usually this happens when the female is between the ages of one and two years old. Several males follow the female for days or even weeks, each one trying to convince her to choose him.

This is a very important decision for the female. She must choose a male who will be a good mate and father. She will depend on him to bring her food when their pups are very young and she is unable to leave them to hunt for herself. Later, he will bring food to the pups, too, and will help raise them.

A female coyote playfully bites the ear of her mate.

Mating coyotes will have a family in 60 to 65 days. This pair is wearing radio collars so scientists can keep track of where they go.

When the female decides which of the males courting her will be her mate, the other males leave. Many of them will not find a mate and will be alone for the rest of the year.

The female and her new mate travel, hunt, and sleep together. They breed any time from late December to February. Their pups are born 60 to 65 days later.

While the pups are growing inside her, the female prepares as many as a dozen dens. She finds old burrows once used by badgers or other animals and removes any debris left by the original owners. If the den isn't large enough, she digs out more soil. Her finished den has a narrow tunnel from 5 to 30 feet (1.5 to 9 m) long, with an enlarged area at the end that may be 5 feet (1.5 m) across and 5 feet tall.

Biologists think coyotes prepare several dens so they can move their family if their first den becomes wet from rain, infested by fleas, or discovered by humans. Coyote parents have been seen carrying young pups in their mouths to a new den as far as 5 miles (8 km) from the pups' birthplace.

Other members of the pack rarely come near the den until the pups are several weeks old. If pack members get too close, the alpha female may chase them away. Instead, they gather to play and rest at a **rendezvous** (RON-day-voo) **site,** a tree-lined area up to ¼ mile (0.4 km) from the den. From this site, they communicate with the alpha coyotes by howling and barking.

Preparing a den

For the first few days of a pup's life, its mother does not leave the den.

RAISING A FAMILY

Coyote pups are born between late February and April. An average litter, or group of newborns, contains five or six pups. A large litter may have as many as twelve pups.

Newborn pups are almost totally helpless. They weigh only ½ pound (225 g). They have short, fine fur and short snouts. Their eyes are not yet open, and they have no teeth. They depend on their parents for all their needs—warmth, food, and protection.

27

The mother coyote stays in the den with her pups for several days. Her mate brings her food. Sometimes he kills a mouse or other small prey and carries it home to her. Other times, he swallows the prey whole when he catches it. When he returns to the den, he **regurgitates** (ree-GUR-jih-tayts), or throws up, the prey for his mate to eat.

Without this help from the father, the mother and their pups probably would not survive. From the time the mother is pregnant until she is done nursing, or providing milk for her pups, she needs twice as much food as at other times of the year. But in late winter and early spring, food can be hard to find. There are fewer mice available, and ground squirrels are still hibernating.

A new mother depends on her mate to find food like this piece of carrion for her and their pups.

The mother nurses the pups for about 2 months. Her milk is very good for them, and the pups grow and develop rapidly. When they are 10 to 12 days old, their eyes open and their baby teeth start to come in.

At 3 weeks of age, the pups have fuzzy, dark brown fur. They have learned how to walk, and they climb out of the den for their first look at the outside world.

When coyote pups first come out of the den, they are clumsy and uncoordinated. They tumble and stagger as they try to chase and wrestle with each other. For a few weeks, they return to the den to sleep, and they still depend entirely on their parents.

At 3 to 4 weeks of age, well-chewed regurgitated food is added to the pups' diet of mother's milk. Both parents now help with feeding, and the pups learn to paw and lick their parents' faces to signal that they are hungry.

As their teeth and jaws develop, the pups become able to handle tougher food. Their parents begin to regurgitate meat that has not been chewed as well. The pups' mother continues to nurse them but also goes off to hunt for herself. The pups are rarely left alone, though. When one parent goes hunting, the other remains near the den to keep an eye on the youngsters. When both parents go hunting, other members of the pack guard the pups.

Waiting for a meal of regurgitated food

This is a dangerous time for young coyotes. The pups spend a lot of time out of the den, where they can be attacked by predators such as badgers and eagles. They have not yet learned to hide, run away, or defend themselves.

Coyote parents and other adult members of the pack protect the pups by watching over them and ordering them around. Even when they are very young,

coyote pups can understand and obey vocal signals. They seem to recognize several instructions, including "Get down and stay still," "Go back to the den," and "Here's food."

These ways of communicating are **instinctive** (in-STINK-tiv). That means the pups are born with the ability to give and understand certain messages.

In other cases, the pups learn by watching their parents and other pack members and trying to imitate them. Over time, they learn about the area around their den and where the good hiding places are. They learn how to stalk prey by trying to sneak up on each other in a game of tag. They get practice chasing and capturing prey when their parents bring them mice that are not dead yet.

The pups also start to hunt for themselves. Their first prey are often grasshoppers. The pups learn to wait patiently for an insect to settle on a blade of grass. Then they approach it quietly and pounce on it quickly. The insects they catch are an important part of their diet. Pups who have lost both parents can sometimes survive on the insects they capture.

A twelve-week-old pup watches intently (above) *before pouncing on an insect* (right). *Soon it will join its parents on hunting trips* (opposite page).

When the pups are 2 to 3 months old, the family moves from the den to the rendezvous site. Here the pups sleep outside with their parents and the rest of the pack. They practice hunting grasshoppers and mice.

In July or August, when the pups are 4 to 5 months old, they join their parents on hunting expeditions. The pups and their parents spend the rest of the summer hunting, playing, and preparing for the coming winter.

These pups are nearly full grown.

By fall, the pups look more like adults. Their snouts have lengthened, and their fur has lightened to a tan or buff color. Their guard hairs have not grown in yet, though, so they lack the distinctive dark or rusty markings of the adults.

Only half of the pups born in the spring survive until fall. Harsh weather, hunger, and diseases such as tapeworm and mange can be hard on young pups. Predators and hunters also take their toll on the pup population.

34

ALL GROWN UP

Of the surviving pups, some drift away from their parents' pack in the fall to start life on their own. These coyotes are called **transients** (TRAN-zee-unts), a word that means "moving." Transient coyotes do not belong to a pack. They roam about, either alone or with one or two other transients, and may sleep in a different place every day. They do not mate or raise pups.

Many coyotes are transients for a year or so. During this time, they may travel as much as 300 miles (480 km) from where they were born. When they get older, they try to find a mate. If they do not succeed, they remain transients. Coyotes who do find mates then look for a territory that will provide them plenty of food and not much competition from other coyotes or disturbance from humans. The mates settle down there and become **residents,** forming a new pack.

This seven-week-old pup, practicing howling (above) and exploring (right), requires the watchful eye of a parent or an older sibling.

While many pups leave their parents in the fall, some stay on, becoming part of the pack that raised them. They may stay in this pack for one or more years or for the rest of their lives. While in their parents' pack, these coyotes do not mate and raise families of their own. Instead, they become **helpers**—baby-sitters for their parents' later litters of pups.

Helpers do everything for the pups that the parents do except nurse them. They hunt, bring back food, and regurgitate it when the pups paw or lick their mouths. They play with the pups and teach them to hunt and howl. Helpers also guard the pups and chase away intruders that threaten their little brothers and sisters.

Biologists who have studied coyotes have found that this baby-sitting helps the parents, the new pups, and the helpers. The parents get help caring for their pups. The pups have more adults to look after them. And the helpers learn a lot about how to raise a family. This seems to make them better parents if they ever do leave home, find a mate, and start a family of their own.

A helper communicates with its young sibling

The older pups' decision to stay in their parents' pack or move far away depends on several things: how much food is available, how many coyotes are already in the area, and whether the humans nearby leave them alone or try to kill them.

In places where people leave coyotes alone, a coyote's average life span is 13 years. They have small litters, and many of the offspring remain in their parents' pack for several years. These packs tend to be large, with up to a dozen adult members.

In places where people are a threat to coyotes, the animals rarely live past age 4 or 5. These coyotes have larger litters, but most of the pups die during their first year. The surviving pups usually leave their parents' territory for safety's sake, so packs remain small. There are also more transient coyotes in such areas.

A bullet hole in this skull tells us how the coyote died.

THE HUMAN THREAT

Huge numbers of coyotes, as well as other predators such as wolves and mountain lions, have been killed by humans since European settlers first crossed North America. The settlers did not know that most coyotes, if left alone, do not hunt domestic animals. They thought these animals would prey on their livestock, so they tried to eliminate predators completely.

The smell of dog food lures a coyote to this home. A meeting between the coyote and the dog could leave one or both animals seriously injured.

The same thing still happens on ranches throughout the United States. But the results are not what people might expect.

When a pack loses several members, it may be unable to kill large game. It must find new food sources that are easier to bring down, such as cows and sheep. Humans respond to the loss of livestock by working even harder to kill the coyotes. In turn, attacks on livestock by the remaining coyotes increase.

Ranchers are not the only people in conflict with coyotes. In recent years, people have built more homes out in the country, only to find they live right in the middle of coyote territory. A pet dog or cat may be lost to a hungry coyote.

Some people think killing all coyotes is the best way to protect themselves and their property. In many states, hunters receive a **bounty,** or sum of money, for every predator they kill. In these states, it is legal to kill any number of coyotes, at any time of year, by any means. Coyotes may be shot on sight, even if they are not bothering domestic animals. Some people make a game of it, shooting coyotes from airplanes or helicopters, or holding contests to see who can kill the most coyotes in a given amount of time.

Above: *Caught in a leg-hold trap*
Left: *A coyote carcass hung on a fence for display*

Another common way people try to kill coyotes is by capturing them in leg-hold traps. Stuck in a trap, a coyote is left to starve to death. But like other kinds of human disturbances, the use of traps often increases the number of livestock attacked by coyotes. This is because many coyotes escape the traps by chewing off the foot or leg that is caught. The lame coyote is more likely than a healthy coyote to attack domestic animals, because it is no longer able to chase down wild game.

An easy way ranchers have found to get rid of a large number of coyotes is to use poison. Poison can simply be put in a deer or cow carcass and left where coyotes will find it and eat it. One-half ounce (14 g) of poison can kill up to 11,000 coyotes!

Poison can also be used by adding it to pellets of animal fat. In the 1950s and 1960s, millions of these deadly pellets were dropped from airplanes over areas where coyotes lived. The smell of animal fat was irresistible to them.

For many years, poisoning was the most popular method of killing coyotes. But people began to complain that the poison killed all coyotes, not just those who preyed on sheep. It also killed other kinds of animals who ate the pellets, as well as the animals who ate the poisoned carcasses of those animals. If a dog ate poisoned bait, it would die. And if a hawk came along and fed on the dog's body, the hawk would die too.

In 1972, the U.S. Environmental Protection Agency agreed that the use of poisoned bait was dangerous. It ruled that poison could not be used on government-owned land. However, it is still legal to use it on private land.

Carrion-eating animals like this bald eagle are put at risk when people leave out poisoned bait for coyotes.

The presence of a guard dog, such as this Great Pyrenees, usually keeps coyotes away.

One common-sense solution to the conflict between humans and coyotes is the use of guard animals. Coyote attacks on livestock happen more often in areas where sheep are left out in remote pastures with no shepherd or guard dog to protect them. Usually if a person or specially trained dog stays with the sheep, coyotes leave them alone. Donkeys and llamas also make good guards. These animals are not timid like sheep and will fight a coyote if the coyote comes too close. Once the coyote sees that, it usually stays away.

Finding meals in garbage cans makes coyotes rely less on hunting and more on humans—and their pets and livestock—for food.

Other sensible precautions are to keep pets and garbage indoors, especially at night, and to avoid hand-feeding coyotes. Some visitors to Yellowstone National Park think it is fun to feed the coyotes who beg along the roads. This practice makes the coyotes less afraid of humans and more likely to attack pets and livestock. Occasionally, these people are bitten by coyotes reaching for food.

In Kansas, a special program has helped people learn to live with coyotes. A biologist named Dr. F. Robert Henderson convinced farmers that coyotes could be helpful to them. More live coyotes meant fewer mice, rats, and rabbits to eat up the farmers' crops. Dr. Henderson proposed trapping or shooting only those coyotes who were caught attacking livestock. All the other coyotes would be left alone, and poison would never be used.

This approach has been very successful for over twenty-five years. It protects farm animals while letting most coyotes live normal, peaceful lives. Farmers win too, because they lose fewer crops to rodents. Kansas has many coyotes but far fewer reports of livestock deaths due to coyotes than states in which coyotes are still hunted.

We still face the question of how to live in peace with the coyote. As in the old legends, they can be seen as both nasty and charming, harmful and beneficial. As we come to understand how coyotes live and why they do the things they do, perhaps we can learn how to respect them and accept them as neighbors.

GLOSSARY

adaptable: able to change to fit the situation

alpha: the name given to the highest-ranking male and female of each pack. The alpha male and alpha female breed each year, while other members of the pack do not breed.

bounty: a fee paid for killing an animal

canine teeth: long teeth near the front of an animal's mouth, used for holding prey and tearing meat

carcass: the body of a dead animal

carnassials: large teeth near the back of an animal's mouth, used for tearing meat

carnivore: an animal that eats mostly meat

carrion: meat from a dead animal

courtship: attempt by a male coyote to convince a female to choose him as her mate

dominant: ranking higher than another

guard hairs: long, coarse hairs in the coyote's coat, often black at the tips, that help keep it dry

habitat: the type of environment in which an animal normally lives

helper: a young adult coyote who stays with its parents' pack to help raise future litters of pups

instinctive: a behavior or ability that an animal is born with

nurse: to provide milk for one's babies

pack: an organized group of coyotes that lives, hunts, and defends its territory together. Members are usually related to the leaders of the pack, the alpha male and alpha female.

predator: an animal that hunts other animals

prey: an animal that is eaten by other animals

range: the geographic area in which a species lives

regurgitate: to vomit, or throw up, food

rendezvous site: a place near the den where pack members meet between hunting trips, and where the coyote family moves when the pups are ready to sleep outdoors

resident: a coyote who belongs to a pack and lives within the pack's territory

scavenger: an animal that eats the bodies of animals it did not kill

territory: the area in which a pack lives and hunts

transient: a coyote who does not belong to a pack

underfur: pale, short, fine hairs in the coyote's coat that help it keep warm

INDEX

ABOUT THE AUTHOR

Cherie Winner has always been fascinated with dogs and their wild relatives. The day she moved to Laramie, Wyoming, she was greeted by the sight of a huge coyote on the highway. Since then, she and her dog, Sheba, sometimes spot them on hikes around home and hear them singing near their favorite campsite in southeast Wyoming. (Her cats, Tucker and Shiloh, don't like to hike or camp.)

Dr. Winner holds a Ph.D. in zoology from Ohio State University. She is a full-time writer and the award-winning author of *Salamanders*, also published by Carolrhoda.